LET YOUR PERSONALITY BE YOUR CAREER GUIDE

LET YOUR PERSONALITY BE YOUR CAREER GUIDE

How to be **Happy**, **Successful**, and **Understood** at Work

SARAH E. BROWN, PH. D.

Copyright © 2016 by Sarah E. Brown, Ph.D.

All rights reserved. No part of this book may be reproduced, distributed, or transmitted in any form or by any means, including photocopying, recording, or other electronic or mechanical methods, without the prior written permission of the publisher, except in the case of brief quotations embodied in critical reviews and certain other noncommercial uses permitted by copyright law.

For permission requests, write to the publisher, addressed "Attention: Permissions Coordinator," at the address below:

Published by
KnowThySelf, LLC
717 North Union Street, #81
Wilmington, DE 19805
www.bookofyou.com

Printed in the United States of America

Library of Congress Control Number: 2016910489

1. Career —business —Job search. 2. Self Improvement —Education. 3.Birkman Method—Assessments

ISBN: 978-0-9891595-2-4

Book Design by AuthorSupport.com

Table of Contents

Introduction vii

CHAPTER 1: *How This Book Came About* 1

CHAPTER 2: *Personality Deconstructed* 5

CHAPTER 3: *The Know Thyself Process®* 23

CHAPTER 4: *Case Studies* .37

    Sarah Brown 37

    Jack Canfield 45

    Kathleen Koch 49

    Liane Hansen 52

    Su Knoll Horty 55

    Peter Grow 58

    Emile Nelson 61

CHAPTER 5: *Where to Get More Help* 65

INTRODUCTION

If you are currently searching for a job, do you know what will make you truly happy?

Do you know what will make you successful?

Do you know what you will need from your boss or coworkers to be understood at work?

If not, read on.

How would you know an ideal job if it were offered to you?

I have a very simple answer for this. The job would bring you happiness because it would allow you to pursue your interests or passions, using your natural strengths. It would also not cause you exceptional stress because most of your on-the-job needs would be met. If you had all this, you would most likely be happy, successful, and understood at work.

Sounds like an ideal or dream job to me. How about you?

This is a simplified definition, and it just may be simpler to put into practice than you think.

Imagine enjoying what you do on a daily basis and being tremendously successful at it. Does that sound impossible?

It is possible.

All you need to know are a few things about your unique personality. I will show you several ways that you can determine what these factors are and give you some examples of how others have used this information to find their dream job or create these conditions within their current job.

CHAPTER 1

How This Book Came About

I have over 15 years of talent management experience with large multinational corporations. During these years, I often saw people landing in the wrong jobs and being miserable. When I would ask these individuals what their ideal job would look like, they could not answer the question. In fact, many said they did not have a clue. They just knew that the job they were currently in was not it.

What I also observed was that some individuals who had coaches were making changes that they needed to become happy at work. They were either changing jobs altogether or making changes in their current jobs to better align with who they were. So I started to study what these coaches were actually doing. I realized that they were discovering what was unique about their clients and then supporting them to make changes that aligned with that uniqueness. This was very powerful stuff but also time consuming and expensive. I started to think about how we could make these insights and support available to everyone.

I had familiarity with a personality profiling instrument, called The Birkman Method®, and I knew that it had been used quite successfully by world-renowned outplacement firms to help individuals identify and then secure jobs that were uniquely suited to their personalities. Many people are familiar with another personality profiling instrument, the Myers-Briggs Type Indicator (MBTI®). I like to call The Birkman Method® Myers-Briggs on steroids. Myers-Briggs categorizes individuals along 4 dimensions and tells them that they are one type or the other. For example, you are either an introvert or an extrovert. In reality, these dimensions are more like continua. Depending on where you fall on the scale, you may look more like some introverts and still be classified as an extrovert. The Birkman Method® takes 9 different dimensions into account by assigning values along a sliding scale continuum. Along with these behaviors, The Birkman Method® adds an interest component— e.g. a measure of what an individual finds happiness in doing. And, finally, it goes on to distinguish an individual's usual behavior from his or her needs. To use MBTI® language, just because an individual usually behaves as an extrovert does not mean that he/she "needs" an extrovert-dependent environment to be most productive and happy.

One of the pluses of The Birkman Method® is the robust amount of data it can capture about an individual, but this complexity is also the biggest challenge to its use. It has historically only been available to a very select audience because it takes a trained consultant to interpret the results and make it relevant in different situations. That makes it both difficult to acquire and expensive.

I am one of those trained consultants, but I have found a way to simplify the outcomes for individuals by doing 2 things:

- Focusing on a specific situation—like finding a job that is a good fit or improving a specific relationship.
- Helping the individual understand his or her most impactful interests, strengths, and motivational needs and how they apply to the situation under discussion.

Using The Birkman Method®, I have developed a means by which individuals can get a personalized book that describes their specific interests, strengths, and needs and how those factors can guide them in the process of making vocational choices.

What I am going to do in this book is share the basic ideas and give you some tips on how you might explore these areas of your personality for yourself, whether you take The Birkman Method® assessment and get a personalized book or not. I will also share real-life examples of personal insights others have gotten from their personalized Book of You™ and what they did as a result.

If you, too, want a personalized book that contains information all about you, I can offer you a special discount offer for one of the Books of You™. See the chapter on Getting More Help.

CHAPTER 2

Personality Deconstructed

It is more about you than about others. You can create a happy work experience, if you know your interests, strengths, and needs.

Dilbert©2010 Scott Adams. Used by permission of UNIVERSAL UCLICK. All rights reserved.

Each of us is unique. That goes without saying.

The various ways in which each of us is unique are so vast that they can be overwhelming. So, let's simplify them to something much more manageable: your unique interests, strengths, and motivational needs. And let's look at them in terms of the results that you desire: to be **Happy**, **Successful**, and **Understood**.

Happy

Let's look closer at what makes you happy at work and what you can do about it. These are your **INTERESTS**—what you like to do and where you prefer to direct your energy. This is the type of activity you would enjoy if pay, prestige, and opportunities were the same. Interests are different from skills or abilities. For example, what might make you happy is beautiful artwork (interest), but you might not be able to paint (skill).

Here is a partial list of the interests I usually ask people to consider. (They are the very same areas that are identified in The Birkman Method® assessment and the areas that are more fully explored in the Book of You™.)

1. Scientific. Are you interested in the theory behind the way things work? Do you find yourself asking **why** a lot?
2. Mechanical. Are you interested in **how** things work? Do you enjoy working with your hands or on tangible hands-on tasks?
3. Musical. Are you keenly focused on sounds and what you hear? Do you love music?
4. Numerical. Do you love numbers? Do you tend to think in terms of numbers or spreadsheets?
5. Artistic. Is the way things look important to you? Do you find yourself paying special attention to the visual aspects of your work?
6. Outdoors. How important is it to you to be outdoors? Do you get anxious if you are indoors too much?
7. Literary. How much do you tend to focus on words? Is reading a favorite pastime? Do you like to write?
8. Process/Systems. Do you like organizing tasks into logical and organized processes and systems?

9. Persuasive. Do you like influencing or convincing others? Do you like selling?
10. Social Service. How important is it to you that you be directly involved in helping another individual?

You can probably begin to see, at this point, that with knowledge of your interests, you can take charge of such things as:

1. Career Selection. Does the job or career you have selected allow you to pursue those areas of interest that are most important to you?
2. Task Assignments. It is not always possible to be in a job that is an exact match for your highest interests. You can, however, find the tasks in your job that most align with your interests and do more of them.
3. Work/Life Balance. Maybe you cannot find a way to pursue all of your interests in the career you choose. You could then pursue some interests through hobbies. You can take immediate steps to ensure that interests are incorporated somewhere in your life, regardless of whether you are able to incorporate them as part of your job.
4. Time Management. By understanding your interests, you can take a look at how a typical week happens for you and then assess whether there is enough time spent on the areas that interest you most. If you conclude that you are not spending enough time on the interests that are important to you, you can make an action plan to create more time for those activities that bring you happiness. This will make a big difference in your degree of satisfaction with your current job. And, creating time to pursue your interests is something you can do immediately.

Book of You™ Example:
Susan's Interests

Here is an excerpt from Susan's Book of You™ describing some of her interests:

- You have a significant level of interest in the theory underlying the way things work.
- You have an above-average interest in the way things look and may therefore be drawn to tasks involving design, the visual arts, etc. It carries with it a liking for strategic or creative thinking.
- You have an above-average interest in what is heard — music, the spoken word, how things sound and may therefore be drawn to tasks involving this. It carries with it a liking for strategic or creative thinking.
- You have a fairly low level of interest in activities involving influencing or persuading other people.
- You have a low level of interest in tasks involving a systematic or structured approach.

What Susan came to understand from this is that she needed to focus more on internal strategic planning roles (liking for design and strategic thinking) and less on roles that involved selling (low level of interest in activities involving influencing or persuading others) and operations (tasks involving a systematic or structured approach). As she reflected on her career, she realized that where jobs had involved a lot of selling or operations, she was less happy than when she was involved in thinking about strategic plans or creating. She had never done product development, but it occurred to her that this might be an option as well.

Successful

Understanding what makes you successful is simpler than you think.

Dilbert©2014 Scott Adams. Used by permission of UNIVERSAL UCLICK. All rights reserved.

What makes you successful at work? In very simple terms, the answer is a work environment that allows you to easily use your **strengths** and mitigates stress. If your **needs** are met, stress will be alleviated.

Let's look at your strengths, first. These are the behaviors that you have developed as a means to be successful. They are how you usually behave and how you show up to the world. It is the combination of these traits that becomes your reputation. Others can usually see these components of your personality, but whether these behaviors are a strength is situation-dependent.

Each behavior exists on a continuum. There are no right or wrong behaviors, and one end of the continuum is not better than the other. For simplicity, let's consider a car analogy and a continuum of large to small. Consider the differences between a Land Rover and a smart® car. One is big, and the other is small. Is one right or wrong? No. They are just different. Depending on the situation, those differences become strengths. For example, if I am driving in a crowded city, like London, I want a small car that is relatively easy to park on narrow, congested streets. I want a smart® car. But if I am driving on rough, unpaved roads in the mountains, I may prefer a Land Rover that will provide stability and comfort. Which car has the strength? It depends upon the situation. In the case of a smart® car, the small size that creates flexibility in movement and parking is a strength in a crowded, busy city such as London. In the case of the Land Rover, there is protection and a comfortable ride. But whether that is a strength is completely situation-dependent. The large size of the Land Rover is not necessarily as effective in London. And the small size and flexibility of the smart® car is not going to be a strength on unpaved, mountainous roads.

In the right situations, your usual behavior is your strength. But in the wrong situations, your behavior can be ineffective, even detrimental. When learning about yourself, it is important to understand what your usual behavior is. You also need to consider the situations in which your behavior will be a strength, rather than a problem.

Here are some examples of behaviors that we might care about when selecting a vocation:

Candid vs. Sensitively Focusing on Feelings. This is what a fellow Birkman Consultant, Dan Perryman, calls the Mr. Spock/Capt. Kirk continuum (Footnote: 1). At one end of the scale is someone like Mr. Spock, who is completely objective, focuses almost completely on the facts, and works on practical solutions immediately. At the other end of the continuum is someone like Capt. Kirk, who is quite warm and receptive to others' feelings. This individual tends to be more emotionally expressive. A person who is closer to the Mr. Spock end of the spectrum, who tends to focus just on the facts, would likely be more successful in a job that depends upon focusing just on the facts—say criminal investigation or perhaps even scientific research. On the other hand, that behavior may not be as effective in a customer service role, where demonstrating empathy for a customer complaint is key to keeping that customer.

Candid vs. Sensitively Focusing on Feelings

Mr. Spock
Objective
Practical and factual
Focuses on tasks

Capt. Kirk
Warm and receptive to emotions
Emotionally expressive
Focuses on individuals

Works Well Alone vs. Enjoys Group Interactions. Some people are very good at working alone or in one-on-one situations. Others thrive on team activities and group involvement. Again, one is not right or wrong. It depends on the situation. Someone who thrives on working with a team will naturally seek out those work situations that afford an opportunity to do so. One can see that there are situations where each trait is a strength. Consider product development jobs that depend on collaboration to ensure that various ideas are incorporated. Someone who thrives while working on a team will be a natural here. On the other hand, that same preference may not work so well for an author.

Works Well Alone Vs. Prefers Group Interactions

Works well on individual assignments
Thinks and reasons independently
Best in one on one situations
Selectively sociable

Communicative in groups
Enjoys group discussions
Likes meeting new people
Enthusiastic about team activities

Works at a Measured Pace vs. Acts and Responds Immediately. My grandfather used to say that there were two kinds of people in the world—those that rush and wait and those that wait and rush. You need only observe my husband and me going to the airport to understand how true this is. I prefer to go to the airport at a measured pace, and I have no problem then waiting for the plane to take off. My husband, on the other hand, would prefer that we go at the very last minute—rushing at the end to make sure we do not miss the flight. Our domestic arguments notwithstanding, neither is really right or wrong. But you can begin to see that these tendencies can be strengths in different vocations. My husband's preferred behavior is going to be very helpful in dealing with crises that require last minute, quick actions. I see this in his chosen profession, events management. Things always go wrong at the last minute, like a power failure or a performer not showing up. He is a master at dealing with these things and actually thrives on doing so. That is not me. I thrive on more measured, plan-ahead type activities. I always say that I am good at planning to avoid problems. He is good at solving the problems that occur regardless. Both are needed, but in different situations.

Pace of Action

Moves at a measured pace
Conserves energy
Plans before acting
Balances action with thought

Physically active
Operates at a high energy level
Acts and responds immediately

In summary, when it comes to your usual behavior, it is important to not only understand what it is but also to figure out the kinds of situations in which it is likely to be a strength, rather than a liability.

Book of You™ Example:
Kris' Strengths

Here is a summary of Kris' strengths from his Book of You™. Note the commentary on the situations in which these usual behaviors are a strength:

- You are frank, direct and straightforward when relating to others one-on-one. This is likely to be a problem

only if you are dealing consistently with more sensitive individuals.
- You are significantly less structured than most other people. You are more inclined to start a project without a firm plan or with just a broad outline. You probably like trying out new ideas. You are strong on initiating new approaches. You are less at home with structured follow-through. You are inclined to underestimate the degree of structure and security that most people need.
- You are low-key in discussion or debate, consensus-oriented, seeking democratically-based rather than imposed authority and direction. While this is an effective style in many situations, it may work less well with those who look for strong direction.
- You are something of an idealist. You think in terms of general benefit rather than individual competitive advantage. Occasionally, problems can arise when you interact with people with strong competitive needs.
- You have a high level of physical energy. You like to be actively involved. You see direct action as the solution to most problems. It's a style that can verge on micro-managing or finding it difficult to leave well enough alone, particularly in the eyes of people with less energy.
- You think in terms of logic rather than feelings. You are oriented towards facts rather than emotion or sentiment. You are not naturally inclined to see the subjective element in your interactions with others.

- You are concentrative. You tend to do your best work when able to focus on one thing at a time. You prefer to impose a minimum of change on yourself and on other people. Some people may regard you as too resistant to novelty and change.

Kris is on the Book of You™ Team, and he has communicated this information clearly to us with the following decisions on his part:

1. He will interact with others as a team for only short periods of time. He will then go back to working one-on-one and concentrating on the underlying technology.
2. When it comes to implementing technical changes that require team action, he will set the overall direction and will attempt to NOT micro-manage. He has made it clear, however, that this is going to be his natural inclination so the rest of us need to tell him when he is overstepping his bounds.

Your usual behavior, however, may not align with what you actually **need** in a given situation. Let's look at the car analogy again. How do you know, by just looking at a car, how much fuel or the type of fuel it needs to operate effectively? There may be some clues such as size or the sound of the engine, but you really do not know until you read the sticker on the car, read the manual, or experience extensive trial and error. (A customized Book of You™ is much like a car manual, in the sense that it succinctly describes an individual's needs and then goes on to discuss how best to take care of those needs.)

It is the same way with our own needs. Our usual behavior does not predict our needs. Let me explain: The way you normally behave does not always let others know what you need from them or how you want to be treated by them. An individual's usual behavior is not a predictor of an individual's needs.

For example, I worked with a woman who spoke her mind and was very direct with our coworkers. She told others exactly how she felt, without sugar coating her thoughts. So, I assumed that was the way she wanted me to communicate with her. I was mistaken. When I spoke to her as honestly and boldly as she spoke to others, she became very defensive and critical towards me. The relationship was strained, and it created a stressful work environment. You can see how a situation like this could be confusing and frustrating.

Why do we need to understand our own needs? Because, if our needs are not met, we will experience stress, and if we experience stress, we are unlikely to use our usual behavior as a strength. If we understand our own needs, we can take responsibility for getting those needs met. We can understand what we need from our coworkers, from our bosses, and from the structure of our tasks. In other words, we can take responsibility for creating the environments that meet our needs. When this happens, it allows us to demonstrate our usual behavior as a strength.

Here are some examples of motivational needs that should be explored (all of which are addressed by the Birkman Method®):

1. Way others communicate with you: Do you need frankness or sensitivity to your feelings?
2. Amount of work: Do you need plenty to do or do you need a lot of time for thinking?

3. Novelty and change. How much routine works for you? Do you need every day to be different?
4. Schedules: How much control do you want over your own schedule? Do you set it yourself or do you produce your best when someone tells you what your schedule should be?
5. Social demands: Do you need freedom from social demands or do you need lots of interactions.
6. Authority: How important is it to know who the boss is? Do you work best when you are that boss?

> ### Book of You™ Example:
> #### Strengths and Needs Do Not Always Line Up
>
> You will see that Ajit shares Kris' strength around being forthright. But look at the differences between Ajit's Strengths and Needs at Work as reported in this excerpt from his Book of You™:
>
> **Ajit's Strengths**
> - You are frank, direct and straightforward when relating to others one-on-one. This is likely to be a problem only if you are dealing consistently with more sensitive individuals.
> - You are friendly and you meet people easily, probably at ease in meetings and group settings. Therefore, you can find it difficult to relate to less sociable people.

> **Ajit's Needs**
>
> - You need to feel the genuine respect of key individuals. You may sometimes feel slighted if people are too direct or terse in one-on-one encounters.
> - You need a certain amount of time alone or in the company of just one or two people. You tend to be demotivated if you are required to interact with larger groups for long periods of time.
>
> What Ajit learned from all of this is that, in order to be really understood by his coworkers, he was going to have to explain to them his needs—both his need to get away and be alone and his need to know that there was genuine respect between the parties.

Stress

So what happens if we don't create the environment we need? We will likely demonstrate stress behavior. Will the car that is running on the wrong fuel buck evenly or buck erratically or just shut down? It is important to understand this and to be on alert for these stress behaviors. We can then identify whether what we would do (if unchecked by self-knowledge) will help us to get our needs met or just create a big mess for us.

Stress behavior, at best, has unanticipated consequences. At its worst, it may not get us what we want or need at all.

Here is an excerpt from my own book to explain:

> **Sarah's Needs and Stress Reactions**
> - You need a certain amount of time alone or in the company of just one or two people. You tend to be demotivated if you are required to interact with larger groups for long periods of time.
> - You prefer that others are forthright and open with you in one-on-one relationships. You may feel uncomfortable, when others are overly solicitous or too revealing about themselves.
> - You can ignore or overlook the need for meetings and other group activities. You may appear unsociable or remove yourself from general social interaction.
> - You may become overly sensitive to real or imagined criticism. You may feel or appear embarrassed by your errors or mistakes, even if these are trivial.

So, in the first example, we can see that I have a need for a certain amount of time alone. If I do not get it and go into stress mode, my most likely behavior, unchecked by some awareness, would be to overlook or avoid meetings. It might get my need met, temporarily, but it could have the unintended consequence of also communicating that I am completely unsociable. So I need to be careful about this stress behavior. I need to have my need met, but I want to make sure I am not sending signals that are not accurate and/or counterproductive.

Here is the really interesting thing about the second example. What I really need from others is that they be straightforward and forthright with me. But under stress, you can see that I will have a tendency to behave differently. When I think individuals are "beating around the bush" with me and not giving it to me straight, which is my need, I experience stress. And my most likely stress reaction is to be overly sensitive. I can cry much too easily or even explode in frustration. This becomes very confusing to people, as it is not my normal mode of operation. If they then react to my stress behavior and become overly solicitous or start to keep things from me, things only get worse. They are then behaving in the exact opposite way of what I expect and need. My stress experience can increase, and my stress behavior can even increase. It becomes a vicious cycle. We want or need one thing, but we communicate something different, which only gets us more of what we do not need.

Understood

How you are treated is up to you. Have you made yourself understood?

DILBERT © 2005 Scott Adams. Used by permission of UNIVERSAL UCLICK. All rights reserved

The final condition for being in a dream job is for you to be understood.

Typically, we don't succeed alone. We need help from others in a host of different ways. We need interviewers who can help us to determine whether a given job opportunity is the right match for our skills and abilities. We need bosses who can guide us in using our strengths to contribute to the company's success. We need coworkers who will interact with us in a manner that allows us to use our unique strengths and meet our personal needs. We want coaches and mentors who can help us avoid the pitfalls that come from our stress behavior.

Back to the car analogy: Someone who has never met you is unlikely to know what your usual behavior is or the situations in which that behavior will be a strength. So you need to develop a "car sticker" that tells others what your strengths are and what fuel you need to do a job. But what you say needs to be constructed in a way that will encourage people to buy your car.

On the other hand, if you have been working with people for a long period of time, you don't need the introductory car sticker. What you need are warning signs and reminders of how you want and expect to be treated. Think of these as turn signals and brake lights. Going back to the stress example from my own book, imagine what might be different if I had a warning sign that I held up when I was feeling stress that said:

Now, this would only be appropriate with a group that knows me well and in a situation where we had an agreement as to why we were doing this. But an approach like this might actually help me to get my needs met better than the alternative.

What you share with others is situation-dependent. What you say in an interview for a new job is likely to be different than what you communicate to someone with whom you have worked for many years. It is important to think about each situation and craft the car sticker, turn signal, or brake light that describes you precisely.

CHAPTER 3

The Know Thyself Process®

Others can help us take knowledge and convert it into insights for action, but we should choose those people carefully and follow a specific process.

DILBERT © 2013 Scott Adams. Used by Permission of UNIVERSAL UCLICK. All rights reserved.

How do we take knowledge about your interests, strengths, and needs and translate that into actions that will land you in a job that is right for you? The Know Thyself Process® is a simple, 3-step process for developing insights about yourself, incorporating them into your thinking, and helping you determine which actions to take as a result of those insights:

1. KNOW. Take a little bit of information about you, and think about how it applies to the situation you are addressing.
2. TEST. Test these insights with another individual. Why do we test insights? This is like test-driving a car. You would not typically buy a car without some kind of test drive. Testing your knowledge, before you take action, is just like test-driving a car. It allows you to explore this new knowledge in a safe environment and try out possible courses of action, as a result. I think it is best to test this with another individual—someone who knows you and cares about you. That individual can then help you see your blindspots and also think through the potential impacts of potential actions.
3. GO. This part is very important. The sooner you act on new knowledge, the more it becomes useful to you, and the more likely you are to remember it.

Book of You™ Example:
Jane's Coach During TEST

Jane decided to work with a friend as her coach. She used this excerpt from her Book of You™ to both select that person and establish the guidelines that they would follow, as she shared her insights and tested potential actions:

- You prefer your partner to be direct and open with you.
- You need to feel confident that the relationship between you and your partner is private.

- You will be most effective when you and your partner work within broad rather than highly-defined guidelines.
- You need to feel that your partner will not be afraid to discuss openly any differences in opinion between you.
- You need to feel that you and your partner will benefit in concrete ways from the work you do together.
- You need to feel that you and your partner are addressing issues of real importance, and that you are both committed thoroughly to the work you are doing.
- You need to feel that you have your partner's full attention when you are talking about serious matters.
- When your partner expresses unusual or unorthodox opinions, you can find it stimulating.

The trick, of course, is coming up with that initial piece of knowledge about yourself. In this case, it is knowledge of your interests, your strengths, and your needs. Let's look at each component and some ways that you can identify what your interests, strengths, and needs are, as well as how you can work with a partner to increase your happiness and success in a current job.

To get us started, it might be helpful to consider a few roles that you already have, such as your current job and/or volunteer roles. List them here and note how happy, successful, or understood you feel in each role. You can rate these as high, medium, or low. For example, if you are very happy in a role, mark High under happy. If you are not at all happy in that role, rate it Low.

Role Analysis

List roles and indicate how happy, successful, and understood you feel in that role (H, M, L)

Role	Happy	Successful	Understood
Student			

INTERESTS

KNOW.

As a reminder, interests are activities about which you are passionate. You enjoy doing these things on a daily basis. You do not necessarily have to be skilled at these, although people often develop skills in these areas because they enjoy doing them and have spent so much time doing so. For example, you may love music and spend lots of time listening to music every day, but you may not be able to play a musical instrument or even sing well.

There are several ways that you can get a handle on your interests, but it is important to understand that you are the best source for determining what your interests are. Even if you take an assessment to determine what your interests are, you are supplying the input. So, you can make a very good start at this by just taking a few minutes to sit quietly and write down everything that comes to mind. Do not limit your brainstorming to just activities that you think are relevant to a job. If you like the outdoors, for example, write that down. If it is really a passion for you, you will need to find a way to satisfy it, either on the job or off, so it is important to capture it now.

If you need a little help getting started, consider this quick test, which I adapted from the interest categories measured by the Birkman Method®. On a scale of 1-10, with 10 being "I love it" and 1 being "I hate it," score each of these areas in terms of how important they are to you. Label everything that you score as 7 or higher as a passion and everything that you score a 3 or lower as an aversion. One of the things that you will want to do to be happy is to maximize the amount of time you spend on your passions and minimize the amount of time you spend on your aversions.

Interest Quick Test Part 1

Name	Description	Rating (1-10)	Passion/Aversion
Scientific	Are you interested in theory? Do you ask "why" a lot?		
Mechanical	Are you interested in "how" things work? Do you enjoy working with your hands?		
Musical	Are you keenly focused on sounds and what you hear? Do you love music?		
Numerical	Do you love numbers? Do you think in terms of numbers and spreadsheets?		
Artistic	Is the way things look important to you? Do you pay special attention to the visual aspects of what you are doing?		

Interest Quick Test Part 2

Name	Description	Rating (1-10)	Passion/Aversion
Outdoors	How important is it to be outside? Do you get anxious if you are indoors too much?		
Literary	How much do you focus on words? Is reading a favorite pastime? Do you like to write?		
Process/Systems	Do you like organizing things? Is working with processes and systems fun?		
Persuasive	Do you like influencing or convincing others? Do you like selling?		
Social Services	How important is it that you be directly involved in helping another individual?		

TEST.

Now that you have this list, let's look at your current roles and see just how much you are working with your passions and avoiding your aversions. Star anything that you feel is being completely satisfied in your current job. For those items that are not starred, identify the ones that you are satisfying outside of work. What you have left is a list of interests that are not currently being satisfied. Do the same thing with your aversions. This is what you want to TEST with someone else. Show him or her this list, and explore ideas that come to mind about what you could do to increase your ability to entertain this interest. Here are some examples:

1. Outdoor interests. Can you move your desk closer to a window? Can you have lunch outside? Can you hold a meeting or take a call while sitting on the porch?

2. Persuasive. Can you volunteer to participate in a sales call or prepare material for one? Can you test a proposed process change by trying to convince a colleague of its importance?
3. Social Service. Can you find a volunteer role with a nonprofit that will help you feel that you are giving back and serving the needs of others?
4. Finally, circle all those that you and your TEST partner think you could begin to implement now.

GO.

Identify something you can do in the next week to make an improvement in your current situation. Schedule it, and do it. Then, make a list of things that need to be incorporated into your next role or job.

STRENGTHS

> *"Most people think they know what they are good at. They are usually wrong . . ."*
> **—PETER DRUCKER,** Business Guru

KNOW.

As I have said before, I think it is most helpful to start this list by asking others what they think. (Taking an assessment may be faster, but even then you may want to discuss the results with others.) They will give you some insights that you may have never even considered. Then, you can expand this list with ideas that you have, as well. One caution here: I would not ask a spouse or partner. They will often tell you what you are NOT good at, and that will get you off track and focused on the wrong things.

Here is a quick test you can use to get you and your test partner started. It is adapted from the work of Dr. Roger Birkman and Birkman International.

For each question, decide whether it is true or mostly true about you and check the appropriate box. Then, for each part, add up the number of true responses and the number of false responses.

Remember when I said that strengths were situation dependent? Well, these behaviors are going to be strengths only in certain situations. To give you a jump start on the kinds of jobs in which your usual behavior is likely to be deemed a strength, just add up the number of trues and falses and circle the line in the chart below that summarizes your answers:

Strengths Quick Test Part 1

Item	Description	TRUE	FALSE
1	Argue when contradicted		
2	Openly express differences of opinion with groups and individuals		
3	Argue a point when I know I am right		
4	Tell a person what I think of him when annoyed		
5	Bluff to get what I want		
6	Put annoying people in their places		
7	Help friends by pointing out their faults		
8	Keep others guessing		
Total			

Strengths Quick Test Part 2

Item	Description	TRUE	FALSE
1	Like firm and strict supervision		
2	Orderly and systematic		
3	Seldom leave things until the last minute		
4	Want to be early for appointments		
5	Work for accuracy rather than speed		
6	Like to finish a job I've started even though others lose patience with me		
7	Can schedule my time for a week or longer and stick with it		
8	Prefer to take care of the details rather than take things as they come		
Total			

Strengths Quick Test Results

Part 1 True Answers	Part 2 True Answers	Work Type	Examples
5 or more	5 or more	Production centered	Manufacturing
4 or fewer	5 or more	Procedure centered	Accounting
5 or more	4 or fewer	People centered	Sales
4 or fewer	4 or fewer	Idea centered	Strategic Planning

TEST.

What should you do with this list? I think the most helpful thing to do is to TEST these characteristics with a partner to determine the situations in which they are actually strengths, rather than liabilities. Show him or her these charts, and see if (s)he agrees with your assessments of your behavior. Then, explore other possible job choices where your strengths might be utilized.

GO.

As an immediate first step in the job search process, I suggest that individuals think about how they incorporate their strengths into the process. For example, if individuals have strengths in working with groups, they can immediately engage a group in the search process itself. You will see in the case study about Peter that this is exactly what he did. This not only reinforced for him what his strength was, it made the process easier because he was acting from a strength. The next important step, however, is to start developing the car sticker that can be used to communicate what you are naturally good at. This becomes a part of your selling message of who you are and why you are right for the job.

NEEDS

KNOW.

Needs are often hidden from others and even from ourselves. Many people think it is selfish to think about our own needs but, in reality, we all have them and, if we do not recognize them and address them, they come back to haunt us. We would never think it is selfish for someone to need food or water. Motivational needs are much the same thing. There is a reason why airlines tell us to put our own mask on before helping others. If we cannot breathe, if we are experiencing stress, we are not free to help another person because we will become too focused on our own need to breathe or survive.

I think the best way to uncover these needs is through an assessment but, if that is not available, the next best thing is to think about times that you were under stress and examine the causes of that stress. This is the approach I took when I was initially trying to understand myself, and it is what I share in the first case study. Here are some examples of how this analysis may proceed:

I had a client presentation due Wednesday. Tuesday night, I still did not have the presentation complete nor did I have all the materials. I had to work all night to be ready. I felt a lot of tension in my body. My head ached. Underlying need: to not work under deadline pressure.

My boss ignored my comments in a meeting. I felt marginalized and inadequate. Underlying need: to be validated by others.

I attended an all day group meeting. At the end of the day, I was absolutely exhausted. Underlying need: to have some alone time.

It is important to note that different people will have different reactions to the very same situations. Some people are energized by working at the last minute and are drained by working on something too far ahead of time. Some people have absolutely no reaction to having comments ignored in a meeting. Some people are absolutely energized by group meetings. There is no right or wrong answer in any situation. The clue is to determine whether you feel stress and, if so, what your underlying need may be.

TEST.

In the test phase for needs, the important thing to do, with a partner, is to explore whether you have identified the right need and then determine whether there is an alternative way to get the need met. But it is extremely important to think this through with someone else, BEFORE you take action on it. You want to anticipate all of the potential implications of action and, frequently, we cannot do this by ourselves.

GO.

So, what would be an immediate action you can take with your initial understanding of needs? Similar to the way we discussed strengths, you can look at what is likely to cause stress in the job search process and find ways to explore that. The important step, however, is to start writing down what will be required in the job environment to minimize your stress. You can then develop questions that you want to ask in the interview to find out whether the environment is going to be right for you. This is a very empowering way to own your needs.

Communicating your needs appropriately takes some thought and practice.

DILBERT © 2014 Scott Adams. Used by Permission of UNIVERSAL UCLICK. All rights reserved.

Book of You™ Example:
Joan's Ideal Work Environment

This is an excerpt from Joan's Book of You™ describing her in the ideal work environment that would keep her motivated and stress-free:

- Likely to be more self-motivated when you are not made to specialize in a particular area of work.
- Responds readily to opportunities to influence others directly.
- Particularly responsive to situations where helping others is involved.
- Motivated by projects where visual appeal is important.
- Enjoys working with documentation or documenting processes.
- Likes projects which involve the spoken word or which have an auditory component.
- Prefers direct, no-nonsense instructions and encouragement.
- Level of self-motivation is increased by popular support.
- Prefers a minimum amount of rules and procedures.
- Considerably self-motivated by incentives directly linked to performance.
- Is more self-motivated when permitted to schedule herself.
- May need emotional support if feeling reluctant to perform

- Needs the opportunity to be a little unorthodox on occasion.
- Should not be forced to make fast decisions.
- While able to relate to the typical larger corporate structure, can feel comfortable to some extent in smaller, less centralized entities.
- You tend to be motivated primarily by the inherent interest you have in work or in its results, rather than by work for its own sake.
- You are motivated by typical corporate values and ethics.

Joan used this information to actually craft a job working for herself. That gave her sufficient freedom and control over her work and schedule, as well as the opportunities to do things differently. She realized, however, that she needed the support of others, too, so she takes on projects that allow her that type of interaction.

CHAPTER 4

Case Studies

As we go through a few case studies, I am going to share with you how these individuals have sought to develop knowledge of themselves and translate that knowledge into a vocational direction. Each case study will describe a different tool and approach that you can use in the process.

Sarah Brown

Approach: Use a decision flow chart and find your niche.

We will start with my story. I am going to share with you a tool that is appealing to my analytical nature. You can use it to reflect on your own career journey. To use it, think about a major decision you made in the past about your own career. In the gray triangular box, list the decision you were pondering. The choice you made gets labeled on the blank arrow. The choice or choices you did not make go where the NOT arrow is.

Now, reflect on what you were consciously deciding when you made that choice. What were you aware of? Was it an interest, a strength, or a need? What was the result? Were you happy? Were you successful? Were you understood or in constant stress?

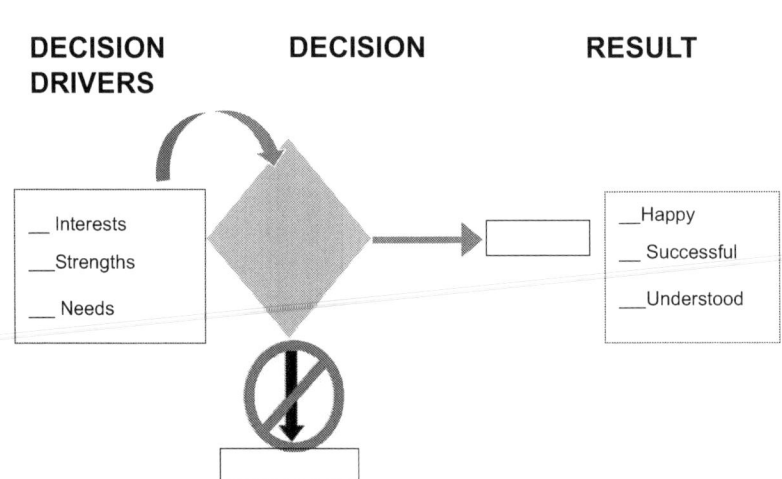

Let's take an example from the beginning of my career. I have always had a fondness for mathematics. In fact, that was my major in college. I cannot honestly say that I was conscious of the reasons I chose math, but I understand now that it played to one of my keen interests. One of the first big decisions that I can remember making was whether to specialize in theoretical work or go into applied work (e.g. computers). Here is a depiction of that decision:

Sarah's Career Journey

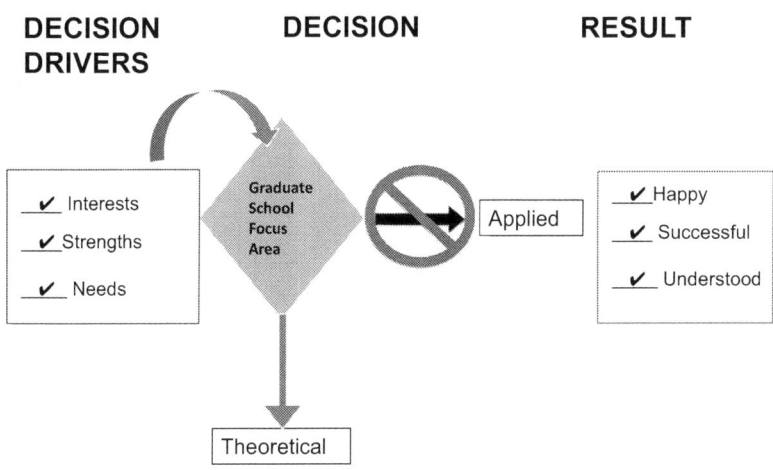

When I reflected on that decision, I realized that I made it with the following considerations:

1. I liked the thought processes associated with theoretical math much better than the hands-on work of computer, or applied, math. This was playing to my interest.
2. In theoretical math, one spends a lot of time "thinking" about concepts and concentrating on logic. This played to two of my strengths: I thrive on conceptual thinking, and I am highly concentrative.
3. As a graduate student in this area of mathematics, I spent equal time alone, one-on-one with my faculty advisor and research partner, and in a classroom. This played to my needs for a balance of time alone and with a few others.

The result was that I was very happy. In fact, the year I worked on my master's degree was probably the happiest of my life. I was very successful. I finished my master's coursework and my thesis faster than anyone had in the past, and my thesis became a published work in my field. Lastly, and importantly, I felt no stress. It truly was a blissful year for me.

When I look back on my career, I realize that I was happier that year than I have been at any time in my career, since then. That is, until just recently. Let's look at how a few more decisions played out.

It had been my intention to continue and get my Ph. D. in theoretical math so that I could teach and do research at the university level. That would have been a good choice for me. I realize that now because teaching is a profession that is well aligned with my interests, strengths, and needs.

BUT, at the time I was finishing my master's degree and considering where I would go to work on my Ph.D., I did a market scan. It is hard to believe but, at that time in the mid-1970s, the market had too many

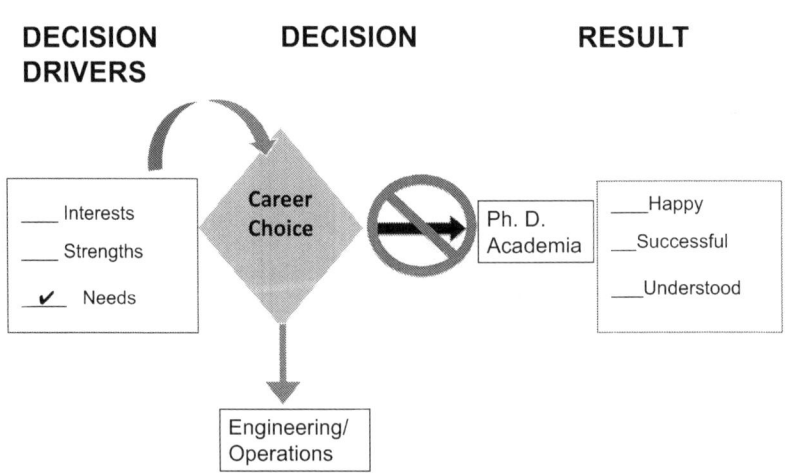

Ph.D. theoretical mathematicians. There were many recent graduates who were waiting on tables, while waiting to get an academic appointment. I did not think that I needed more education, if I wouldn't be able to apply it to my chosen field. Plus, I needed money with which to live.

So, I made my next big decision: I decided to scrap graduate school and go into business to earn as much money as I could.

I was aware of only one thing: I wanted predictability in my environment and a secure income, which is a real need for me. So I chose to take a job with the Bell System, as an engineer, working in telephone central office operations. There could have been much better choices for me. This kind of operations job required a lot of hands-on, applied work. This is not my interest. It also required me to work with lots of people. This is not my strength. The result: I was not happy; I was not particularly successful; I was definitely not understood by my bosses and coworkers. This created stress, which only fueled my unhappiness.

There were many other choices that may have been better for me, at this time. For one thing, I could have gone into teaching at the high school level and waited until the market was more favorable. Another choice that I briefly considered was to teach math at the Navy's nuclear propulsion school.

This experience, however, points out something that I think is important to understand. Even if you are not in the ideal job, you can do things to make improvements in your situation so that you are happier, more successful, and better understood. It is called "finding your niche." And this is exactly what I did.

I knew that I was never going to excel in this operations environment, but there was an area where I could excel and create my niche: Digital telephony was just beginning to come into play. It was already being used extensively in carrier technology and toll switching, but it was not yet being used in local central office equipment. All of this technology relied on relatively new computer technology to operate, and the software behind it was not well understood. I realized I could specialize in that. It was much more conceptual in practice than any of the other areas I had been involved with, and it interested me. (This particular work was even more conceptual than most other areas of computer and software work, as well.) It was also work that required a lot of concentration and thought. This played to my strengths.

The result: I was very successful in this role. I also created a very good reputation for myself. But I cannot say that I was terribly happy. Why was that? Well, my needs were not met. Because of the nature of the work I was doing, I had to do a lot of the work at night, so as not to disrupt customers who were placing telephone calls during the day. So I worked at night and slept during the day. That did not give me any

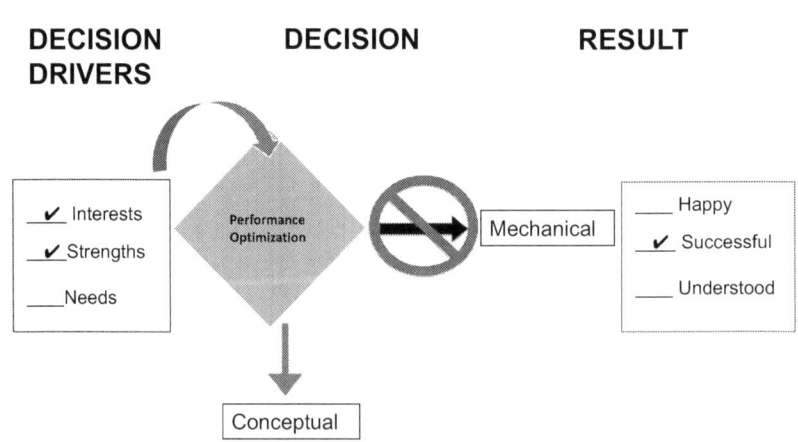

time to enjoy the outdoors, which is such an interest for me that it is also a need.

I will fast-forward now to my most recent career decision. I was working for Accenture, as managing director responsible for Accenture's Business Process Outsourcing work for all of its retail clients in North America. I had achieved a lot in my career, and, by most external standards, I was successful. But I was not completely happy and, most importantly, I was stressed all the time.

This time, I had full knowledge of my interests, strengths, and needs so I looked carefully at the causes of my discontent and what I could do about them.

I looked at my interests first. In my role at Accenture, was I pursuing things that interest me? The answer was a partial yes, but I was spending more of my time on existing operations than on creative conceptual work that could bring new value to our clients.

Looking at my strengths, I was using a lot of my strengths, but I was also spending most of my day on group conference calls. This left little time for me to use my most successful behaviors—concentrating and thinking alone.

The real key for me was a realization about my needs. As my grandfather used to say, there are two kinds of people in the world: those who wait and rush and those who rush and wait. I rush and wait. I like to get things done early so that I do not feel any deadline tension. Accenture is very much a wait and rush kind of culture. I had trouble getting attention on a client issue until just before it was needed. This caused me to have to work hurriedly, at the last minute or late at night, to ensure we were ready for client interactions. This did not play to my needs and kept me in constant stress. I realized that I need to be in total control of my schedule to address this need.

There is one other need that was not being addressed. This gets at the value component of needs that I talked about earlier. I was not satisfying my values around individual growth and development. I had always "felt" that the best contributions I could make to the world were to enable others to learn and grow so that they could also contribute more to the world. This value was not being completely satisfied in my role at Accenture.

So, I combined all of this knowledge about my interests, strengths, and needs (including values) and decided to retire from Accenture and start my own business. This allowed me to share these insights with others and satisfy my needs and desires at the same time.

The result so far: Fabulous! Now, that is not to say there have not been some challenges. There have. But I can analyze the challenges in terms of my interests, strengths, and needs and then decide what to do.

Overall, I have not been this happy since I was in graduate school 30 years ago.

Career Journey

DECISION DRIVERS	DECISION	RESULT
✔ Interests ✔ Strengths ✔ Needs	What Else is there? → Start own business ⊘ Continue in current role	✔ Happy ✔ Successful ✔ Understood

Jack Canfield

Author of *Chicken Soup for the Soul* and *The Success Principles*

Approach: The Life Purpose Exercise

My hero is Jack Canfield. He has taught me a lot about writing, marketing, taking risks, and following your dream. It was one of the biggest privileges of my life to participate in a MasterMind retreat at his home in November of 2015. While I was there, he suggested that I rename my customized books to the Book of You™. That is exactly what I did. You can see an interview we did at that retreat on my website: bookofyou.com. I have read and studied most of what Jack has written over the years, and I think he has a lot to teach about developing self-knowledge and using it to become happy and successful.

Jack Canfield's book *The Success Principles* has been published in 30 languages and read in over 108 countries. He studied these principles for close to 40 years and practiced them in his own life, overcoming many challenges in the process. He was raised by an alcoholic mother and a workaholic father. He put himself through college and graduate school. When he wrote his first book, *Chicken Soup for the Soul,* it was rejected by 144 publishers before it was finally accepted by one. It went on to sell over 125 million copies. Nothing was handed to Jack. He had to create everything from scratch. Using these success principles, he has now written more than 200 books, including 60 *New York Times* bestsellers. He has apppeared on every major talk show in America. He has a thriving training business and commands $60,000 for speaking engagements with Fortune 500 companies. He is called America's #1 Success Coach. He knows firsthand that these principles work.

In addition, over more than a decade, he has also received lots of feedback and heard success stories from readers and individuals in his training programs so he knows that these principles work for others, as well.

The book *The Success Principles* contains 67 different principles, but I am commenting here on Success Principle Number 2: BE CLEAR WHY YOU'RE HERE. Jack believes each of us is born with a life purpose. Discovering this purpose and being true to it is probably the most important thing you can do, if you want to be truly happy and successful. In fact, Jack's definition of success is fulfilling your soul's purpose. He goes on to say that, if each of us would do this, there would be no unmet needs in the world. Everyone wins when YOU are "on purpose."

To quote from the book, "To be 'on purpose' means you're doing what you love to do, doing what you're good at, and accomplishing what's important to you." In other words, we just need to tap into our essence to understand what our purpose is. Jack explains that we cannot be born with a dream or purpose and not also have the capacity to fulfill that purpose.

Looking at the life of Jack Canfield, it's clear that he had a pretty good idea of what his life purpose was when he first started teaching in Chicago after finishing college. He knew then that he had a passion for teaching and inspiring others, but he continued to refine that understanding for himself by attending countless personal development workshops. He read every book he could get his hands on that might help him with his personal understanding. He spent and continues to spend a considerable amount of time each day in personal reflection and meditation. As he said recently on Oprah Winfrey's SuperSoul Sunday series, "I know now that my purpose is to inspire and empower people to live their highest vision in the context of love and joy."

Jack includes in his book several exercises that help individuals develop clarity about their life's purpose. One of these exercises, which I include here, is The Life Purpose Exercise, which he adapted from a similar approach in Arnold M. Patent's book *You Can Have It All*. It takes a lot of time and good thought, but I encourage everyone to do this kind of reflection.

What Jack has noted and what I see so often in my work are the same thing. Too often, people have trouble answering questions 1 and 2 of The Life Purpose Exercise: what they are good at and what they are passionate about. What you are passionate about is what I call interests. What you are good at is what I call strengths. In addition to The Life Purpose Exercise, you can visit www.successprinciples.com/resources to find some additional exercises and pointers to sources that can help you explore the answers to these questions.

Jack Canfield believes you will be Happy and Successful, if you are "on purpose." I think he would add the following, as well: While it is great to be Understood, that may wind up being less important to you, when you experience the joy of being who you were born to be.

*The Life Purpose Exercise**

List two of your unique personal qualities, such as *enthusiasm* and *creativity*.

_____

_____

List one or two ways you enjoy expressing those qualities when interacting with others, such as *to support* and *to inspire*.

_____

_____

Assume the world is perfect right now. What does this world look like? How is everyone interacting with everyone else? What does it feel like? Write your answer as a statement, in the present tense, describing the ultimate condition, the perfect world as you see it and feel it. Remember, a perfect world is a fun place to be.

_____

_____

_____

_____

Combine the three prior subdivisions of this paragraph into a single statement.

_____

_____

Example: My purpose is to use my creativity and enthusiasm to support and inspire others to freely express their talents in a harmonious and loving way.

Shared by Jack Canfield. Adapted from The Life Purpose Exercise from Arnold M. Patent, *You Can Have It All*.

Kathleen Koch

Best-Selling Author
Founder of LeadersLink
Former CNN Journalist

Approach: *Use an unanticipated setback to examine your passions and strengths, then face your fears and go for it.*

On the surface, Kathleen Koch seemed happy with her career at CNN. She had even convinced herself that she was happy. Kathleen had reached what many would consider a pinnacle: For 14 months, she had been a White House correspondent, after years in Washington covering everything from the Pentagon and Capitol Hill to aviation and disasters. But, deep down, Kathleen knew she was not satisfied.

Then, in 2008, she was caught up in layoffs at CNN. Kathleen was shocked and confused but, as she examined her thoughts and emotions more carefully, it became clear that she had not really been happy. Kathleen realized that she could use this turn of events as an opportunity to do what she really wanted to do. But what was that?

Here is what she knew: Ever since Hurricane Katrina took its toll on her hometown on the Mississippi Gulf Coast, Kathleen had been more drawn to disaster-related stories. She was really interested in the long view—the many years and hard road to recovery. Kathleen was fascinated with how individuals survived and how they changed in the process. She knew that those stories could be a means for inspiring others.

When Kathleen looked at her strengths, she knew she could write well. She also knew that she was a good interviewer. Interviewing involved not only finding and connecting with people, but also winning their trust and coaxing the story from them. She was skilled at all of this.

Kathleen sensed that there was a book rattling around in her head. On the other hand, she had never written a book. It was a daunting enterprise. This is where facing her fears squarely and moving on anyway came into play.

She used her writing skills to craft a book proposal, complete with sample chapters that her agent submitted to every major publisher in New York. They were all rejected. The typical response? "We love learning about Mississippi's untold hurricane story. We love your characters. We love the way you write. But Katrina books just don't sell well."

Kathleen could have easily given up. Instead, she looked at the resilience and perseverance of the people of the Gulf Coast that she had covered. These people had refused to quit after Katrina. They were rebuilding their lives. They were growing. She decided she couldn't quit either.

Kathleen had a group of very supportive friends. They brainstormed with her about what to do next. Out of that session came the idea to find a regional publisher. Within a month, she had done just that. Her book, *Rising from Katrina: How My Mississippi Hometown Lost It All and Found What Mattered*, is now an Amazon best seller. It won the 2011 Gold Award for Best Regional Non-Fiction in the South-East from Independent Publisher and honorable mention for 2010 Book of the Year in the Regional Category from ForeWord Reviews.

After this tremendous achievement, Kathleen had to look again at what comes next. TV did not feel right anymore. On the other hand, she did enjoy public speaking, and she was still very passionate about telling the story of recovery after disasters.

Then, Superstorm Sandy struck the East Coast. This was more than just déjà vu. Kathleen felt as if she was watching someone walking down a railroad track about to be hit by a train, and there was nothing she could do to warn them. She realized that the mayors of small Jersey Shore towns would need help and advice from Gulf Coast mayors who had been through Hurricane Katrina so she began facilitating "disaster mentors" to aid in the recovery.

That is when the nonprofit LeadersLink was born, connecting leaders in need with those who have experienced similar disaster-related challenges. Using her interviewing skills, Kathleen has talked with scores of elected officials who are disaster veterans and is in the process of posting their advice on the LeadersLink website. The interactive site will also include a resource hub and a Q. & A. section where leaders can share what they've learned about preventing, preparing for, and recovering from disasters. Drawing on her speaking skills, Kathleen now addresses gatherings of city and county leaders on resilience and the need for a new culture of preparedness. This novel venture has even won support from the United Nations Office for Disaster Risk Reduction.

Kathleen's personal journey has paralleled her hometown's recovery experience. From the devastating layoff in 2008, she has built a new future for herself. As Kathleen puts it, "Sometimes you have to be pushed, kicking and screaming, into growth." She has learned to face her fears and to recognize and use her strengths to follow her passions. Risk can indeed bring reward!

Liane Hansen

Retired award-winning host of various NPR shows

Approach: Leap, and the net will appear.

Liane Hansen had a very successful career with National Public Radio, winning both Emmy and Peabody awards. However, she got into the field somewhat by accident. Her first job out of college was as the secretary to the development director of WSKG, the public radio station in Binghamton, New York. Soon after being hired, the person hosting the morning show was unable to continue. Liane was asked by the general manager if she could step in because she had a great voice. She did, even though she did not know the first thing about being a radio host, and her radio career was launched. Each step of the way after that was a similar experience. Opportunities were presented for which she did not appear to have the experience or credentials; she accepted each opportunity and learned what she needed to learn. She got the job of production assistant on *All Things Considered* and then was asked to host it because no one wanted to work on Christmas. She agreed to host *Fresh Air* for Terry Gross, while Terry was on vacation, and even her once dismissive critics were impressed. When she moved to Washington, D.C., to be with her husband, she became host of a classical music program called *Performance Today*, now on American Public Media. Her final opportunity came in 1989. Up until this time, *Weekend Edition Sunday* had not been a live broadcast, but it was becoming harder and harder to be current and relevant without being live. This is when Liane took over that show, evolved it, and grew it from a listening audience of 200,000 to over three million in 2011, when she retired. Without a doubt, one of Liane's strengths is embracing an opportunity and then learning fast.

In 2011, however, Liane took a step back to examine what she really wanted. She was just completing a divorce from her husband of many years. There was a lot of stress in her life: stress from the divorce, stress from the relentlessness of a weekly show, and stress from dealing with her clinical depression. Liane was tired—tired of the stress, tired of going home to an empty house, tired of working all the time, and tired of D.C. So, when her contract ended, she decided to retire and "follow her bliss" to see where it took her.

The first thing she did was move to Bethany Beach, where she had a beach house. This place had always been a refuge for her, and she loved it. Now, it would be her full-time home. This was an opportunity because she already had the house, but it was also a "leap" because she did not know anyone at the beach.

Someone told her that the best way to meet people in a new town was to either go to church or go the local theater. The latter sounded good to her because she had always enjoyed being a performer. As young as age 5, she knew that she loved singing and dancing. She was active in the drama club in high school and took tap dancing in college. So she began to go to auditions. True to form, she started learning again. She began taking classes at the local Clear Space Theatre Company. She was "following her bliss" to see where it took her. It took her to a host of opportunities—mostly to play characters over 50. She played Sister Margaretta and Frau Schmidt in *The Sound of Music*. She played the minister's wife in *La Cage aux Folles*. She played Evangeline Harcourt in *Anything Goes*. She is having a "blast" with the "bliss."

On the other hand, the pay was certainly not what she was earning at NPR. Nor was it enough to live on. So she had to look to another "bliss," as well. She loved fine dining and had always wondered if she would like the hospitality industry so she decided to "leap" into that to see what she could learn. She found a fine dining restaurant that would "teach" her the ropes, and she is now working part time for them as a hostess. She also went to the local community college and got a tour guide certificate. She is conducting tours at Bethany Beach and is even developing a self-guided tour of the historical houses in the area.

In addition, she is speaking publicly about depression and the toll it can take. She wants to make it more acceptable to discuss. Her TEDx talk on this topic is entitled Reflections from a Functional Depressive and can be viewed at https://youtu.be/zevraXF0dQM

She seems to have found her "bliss." She loves all that she is doing. She has guaranteed sociability in each of these areas of work. Not only is the stress less, she is much less tired. She is making a huge contribution to the Bethany Beach area, with her acting, tour ideas, and hospitality work. She is making a huge contribution to the world, with her work in support of people with depression. And she reports that she can keep her depression at bay because she has work that she loves to do. Comparing how she felt 5 years ago with today is like comparing night to day.

Her advice to retirees? "Just follow your bliss and see what happens. Leap, and the net will appear."

Su Knoll Horty

Artist

Approach: Use leisure activities to explore passions.

A series of articles recently circulated on LinkedIn, in which individuals described "the road not taken," e.g. career paths they did not go down and why. I was fascinated by an article about Mika Brzezinski, cohost of MSNBC's *Morning Joe*, who knew at the very young age of 13 what her passion was and, thus, what her career path should be. She courageously chose not to pursue lucrative paths for which she was recruited, based on that self-awareness, even when times were tough for her. Liane Hansen shares that she had some knowledge of her passions as early as age 5.

It is my experience, however, that many people do not have the clarity of a Mika Brzezinski or a Liane Hansen at such a young age. As you saw in my own story, I certainly did not remain true to my passions. Regardless of age, however, they are discoverable.

Consider the story of Su Knoll Horty. She gained clarity about her passions while doing leisure activities and did not need to approach this question with the analytical precision that I did. Hers was more of a trial and error approach and focused on what she was learning, what she liked, and what she did not like in her leisure activities. She used a process that was very similar to the Know Thyself Process®, engaging a coach to TEST what she was learning about herself and taking action (GO) on new insights. She has been very successful in translating this into vocational direction.

Su had a very successful career in marketing and sales. She sold everything from Volkswagens to high technology Bio Skins. In the late 80s, she began to explore an interest in art by taking a class. This particular class focused on drawing, which turned out to be of less interest to Su than painting. So she dropped the pursuit for another 15 years, as she concentrated on her sales career.

Soon after turning 50, she was encouraged by a friend who shared a similar interest to resume exploration of her passion by taking several more classes. She had an experience that was similar to her first attempt at art, finding that she was not "drawn" to drawing and figurative work. But, instead of giving up again, she began to TEST these observations with her husband. He encouraged her to follow her interest differently and go to an Academy of Fine Arts to take classes in abstract painting. So she did just that. She undertook the GO step and, from that experience, a new career was grown.

She has just completed a month long solo exhibit of her work and has gallery representation. She is not only a regular at juried shows, she has even been a judge at one. She has won numerous awards.

Su emphasizes that her art career builds upon strengths she discovered in her sales career, specifically, a relentless curiosity about what she has engaged in, as well as a disciplined, goal-oriented approach to her work. This curiosity has enabled her to continuously learn about the art world and those who are succeeding in it.

As evidence of this curiosity, Su continues to explore her fascination with colors and evolve her techniques. "The depth and unexpected form that comes from working with intense color is giving me great satisfaction and leading me into intriguing discoveries." Su's latest works offer an intriguing spectacle of color and form, which she calls "Color Pops." Her work can be viewed at suknollhorty.com.

The journey has been one step at a time, with each step leading to a new goal. Throughout, she has TESTed her thinking with her husband and coach.

In summary, Su developed her KNOWledge through her leisure activities. She TESTed it with her husband and coach, and she took action (GO) on what she was learning.

Peter Grow

Approach: A Personalized Book of You™

Perhaps you are somewhere in between Mika and Su in terms of age and self-understanding. Perhaps you know more about what your interests and strengths are NOT than what they actually are. Perhaps you do not want to wait until you are 50 to fully explore this. There is good news for you, as well. There are a variety of tools and assessments available that can assist you in jump-starting the KNOW step of developing this self-knowledge. Here is a sampler:

Free assessments. There are many free assessments online that can help you evaluate what will make you happy and/or what your preferred strengths are. Visit www.authentichappiness.sas.upenn.edu for some simple assessments to measure what makes you happy. Similarly, internet searches of basic personality questionnaires (e.g. MBTI®, DISC®, etc.) will direct you to sites where you can take an abbreviated assessment for free. These tools will definitely get you started on thinking about your strengths. You can also download a free journal from www.bookofyou.com for daily reflection questions that will help you to think about what makes you happy, successful, or understood.

Comprehensive assessments for a fee. Probably the best known comprehensive assessments are MBTI®, DISC®, 16PF, The Birkman Method®, and the Clifton StrengthsFinder. All of these will do a good job of measuring interests and behavioral strengths. I believe that the best one for assessing all three components (interests, strengths, and needs) is The Birkman Method®, and that is why I use it in my books. Except for StrengthsFinder, which is available through a best-selling, semi-customized book, *StrengthsFinder 2.0*, getting the full value from any of these assessments will likely only be realized through a consultation with a trained consultant or in a fully customized self-help application like the Book of You™.

Peter used such an assessment. He actually got a Book of You™ to get started. He discovered that his interests and strengths were pointing him away from his then-current sales roles and toward more technical roles. In addition, this knowledge reinforced something that he already knew deep down—he needed a role that would enable him to work collaboratively with a team, rather than solo, and he worked better when the pace was steady, unlike the roller coaster of activity in sales.

Peter soon got an interview for a more technical project management role. The hiring manager, realizing that Peter had no experience in this type of work, asked Peter why he had come to this particular interview. Peter explained that he had taken the time to completely understand his interests, strengths, and needs and that he had determined that this job was a very good fit for him. He then went on to explain this in more detail. He was offered the job on the spot.

Now, I want to emphasize that this is not typical, but it is an example of what is possible. Peter took the time to understand himself and develop self-knowledge. He focused on that KNOW step, but he will be quick to tell you that he also followed the other steps in the Know Thyself Process®. He also sought out counsel and took full advantage of the TEST phase of the Know Thyself Process®. In Peter's case, his coach was his wife. He tested out every action step with her before actually implementing it. Peter will also tell you that taking some form of action with each piece of knowledge was important, too. A really good first step in taking action on self-knowledge (GO) is to tell your network of friends and colleagues what you are learning and what you are trying to do career-wise, as a result of that learning. This is what Peter did, and this enabled his network to help him get connected with others. In fact, that is what led to the famous interview where he was hired on the spot.

Emile Nelson

Approach: Use The Book of You™ to refine a career plan in college.

Emile was a senior in college when I first met him at a conference for new authors. Emile was helping to market a book on what the Swedes can teach us about leadership. (For more information on that project, check out fikafix.com.) Emile got a Book of You™, on a lark, to give me some ideas on how to better engage college students. The marketer in Emile immediately detected that the book needed to be repositioned for college students.

The other thing that Emile immediately envisioned was how to reach college students. He came up with the idea of enlisting college students who had used this approach to "rep" the books to other college students. He volunteered to be the "sales manager" for this whole effort. All of this happened before I had even seen his personalized book.

But here is the interesting thing: Emile was majoring in English. His primary extracurricular activity was leading his university's newspaper, the *Daily Nexus*. Although he vacillated between going to graduate school for journalism and law school, he had pretty much decided on law school after graduation. His only question was what area of law to specialize in.

When Emile got *The Book of Emile*, he looked carefully at the job families and specific jobs on his companion Career Management Report and noted that roles in the legal field were at the bottom of the list of roles for which he was a match. What was nearer the top were sales management roles and roles that allowed more creative expression via the written word.

Does it surprise anyone that he envisioned the "sales" approach for college students? Does it surprise anyone that he envisioned his role as "sales manager?" It is not surprising to me, at this point.

But what about that yearning for law? Does this rule out a law career for Emile? Should he scrap this whole field because his report suggests he is not a good match? Could he ever be happy in law?

We talked about this at some length, and the answer is that the legal field is not out of the question. But it will be highly important to find the right niche in the legal field. The right role for Emile will involve the use of the written word in some form of creative expression, to persuade or "sell" others. He would need to be a high profile lawyer using the law as a means to promote something he is passionate about.

Emile has now decided to pursue a career in writing and speaking, while acting as Sales Manager for The Book of You™. He is currently finishing his first book and actively recruiting sales representatives across the U.S. He has not discarded law as a career path, but he has decided to carefully consider the niche role he will fill, before he invests in law school.

Case Study Summary:

In the case studies we have examined, we have uncovered various tools for determining interests, strengths, and needs. And we have seen how individuals have used this KNOWledge to make career decisions. We have also seen various approaches to the Know Thyself Process®. I tended to work more alone. Su and Peter tended to involve others more in TESTing their insights. But, in all cases, the individuals in these case studies took action (GO) on what they were learning about themselves and translated that into vocational choices that brought them more joy and happiness.

This same outcome is available to you. No matter how you uncover what is unique and special about you, I encourage you to take action on it. If you need more help with that first step (KNOW), take a look at the next chapter.

CHAPTER 5

Where to Get More Help

I think the easiest way to develop self-knowledge and translate it into vocational choices is through a Book of You™. This is what Peter did.

When you get a book, you start by taking The Birkman Method® personality questionnaire. Within minutes of completion, a completely personalized book is delivered to your inbox in PDF, Kindle, or iBooks format. Each guide contains valuable information about you for the KNOW step of the Know Thyself Process®.

But there are valuable tips and tricks for the TEST and GO steps, as well. In the TEST step, there are guidelines for choosing a coach or partner who is right for you, based on your personality type. There are also sample conversation starters to make your work with that individual effective. What's more, if you are like many and really prefer to work alone, you can use the sample test questions yourself, to make sure you are fully thinking things through before you take action.

In the GO step, there are pointers to specific job families that align with your unique personality. This is a good way to jump-start the process of translating self-knowledge into vocational action. There is even an optional special report that suggests specific jobs within those job families, with links into the Department of Labor's database, where you can get more information on the specifics of each job.

Here is an example from Jennifer's Book of You™, showing the job families that are the most likely candidates for her happiness and success:

Career Focus Chart

NAME	DESCRIPTION	SCORE
Computer Mathematical Science	Designing, developing, and maintaining databases, software, hardware, networks, and other information/logic systems. Duties may include collecting/organizing data, computer programming, providing technical support, web design, and configuring communication systems, among other data-driven functions.	10
Sales Related	Selling goods or services to a wide range of customers across various industries. Duties may include selling retail, appliances, furniture, auto parts, medical services, insurance, real estate, financial or consulting services, securities and commodities, as well as other products/services.	7
Education, Training, Library	Teaching/training individuals or groups of people academic, social, or other formative skills using various techniques/methods. Duties may include instructing children, adolescents, adults, individuals with special needs, or other specific within a formal or informal setting, creating instructional materials and educational content and providing necessary learning resources.	7
Engineering Architecture	Applying principles and technology of chemistry, physics, and other scientific disciplines to the planning, designing, and overseeing of physical systems and processes. Duties may include creating, testing, developing, and maintaining tools, machines, electrical equipment, buildings/structures, or other physical entities.	7

Community Social Services	Counseling, rehabilitating, and/or supporting social and psychological matters of individuals, groups, or communities. Duties may include helping individuals maximize their mental and emotional well-being, cope with addictions, and lead healthy lifestyles, as well as providing spiritual, moral, or vocational guidance.	6
Production	Producing, creating, and/or manufacturing a variety of products (e.g., food, lumber, electrical equipment, fabrics, metals, plastics, stones, fuel) through the operating of specialized tools and/or equipment. Duties may include baking pastries, binding books, cutting, shaping, and assembling furniture, assembling electronics, shaping molten glass, fabricating jewelry, welding metal components. ....speciproduction tasks.	6
Farming, Fishing, Forestry	Performing various outdoor activities related to agriculture, horticulture, aquaculture, and/or forestry. Duties may include attending to live farm, ranch, or agricultural animals; planting, cultivating, and harvesting crops, hunting and trapping wild animals, developing, maintaining, or protecting forested areas and woodlands, and/or cutting, sorting, and grading trees for multiple uses.	5
Business Finance	Analyzing and evaluating business/financial information for the purposes of documenting, making recommendations and/or ensuring adherence to business protocol. Duties may include preparing financial reports, developing investment strategies, analyzing general business trends, or assessing risk/liability, to streamline the operations of an organization.	5
Construction Extraction	Performing hands-on work functions related to the building of structures or the removal of materials from natural settings for use in construction or other applications. Duties may include bricklaying, carpentry, masonry, roofing, plumbing, inspecting integrity of structures according to building codes, mining, drilling, and disposal of construction by-products, using specialized tools and equipment.	5
Protective Service	Serving and protecting the best interests of the community, environment, and/or individualsadhering to federal, state, and local laws. Duties may include investigating criminal cases, regulating traffic and crowds, firefighting, ticketing/arresting perpetrators, inspecting baggage or cargo, responding to emergency situations, patrolling designated areas, guarding establishments, and providing other security measures.	4

Life, Physical, Social Science	Applying scientific knowledge and expertise to specific life, physical, or social science domains. Duties may include researching, collecting/analyzing qualitative and quantitative data, conducting experimental studies, devising methods to apply laws and theories to industry and other fields (e.g., mental health, agriculture, chemistry, meteorology, plant and animal life, human behavior and culture).	4
Installation, Maintenance, Repair	Performing hands-on work functions related to the installation, maintenance, and repair of various machinery, systems, vehicles, and other serviceable equipment. Duties may include diagnosing, adjusting, servicing, and overhauling engines, telecommunications and/or security systems heating, vacuuming, and air-conditioning units; and electronics.	4

And similarly, there are some jobs that she may want to avoid:

Office Administrative Support	Providing clerical support within an organization. Duties may include preparing statements, tracking accounts, record keeping, bill collecting, making phone calls, scheduling appointments, entering data, providing customer service, ordering and tracking inventory, handling monetary transactions, among other administrative support tasks.	2
Healthcare Practitioner Technician	Providing medical care and treatment in an effort to achieve optimal mental and physical well-being. Duties may include assessing patient health, diagnosing illnesses, performing surgery, prescribing medication, implementing prevention strategies, conducting/reviewing laboratory diagnostics, and supervising medical support staff. Most of these occupations require a graduate education.	2
Transportation Material Moving	Piloting, driving, operating, or navigating transport vehicles or material moving machinery (e.g., aircraft, automobiles, water vessels, construction cranes, locomotives, tractors). Duties include flying commercial airplanes, directing air traffic, driving public or school buses, taxis, trucks, ambulances, commanding motor-driven boats, inspecting freight and cargo, conducting trains, operating forklifts, among other transportation and material moving tasks.	1

Building/Grounds Cleaning Maintenance	s Cleaning and maintaining hotels, hospitals, offices, and other establishments, as well as landscapes. Duties may include groundskeeping, planting trees, watering plants, housekeeping, washing windows, vacuuming, exterminating pests, among other cleaning and maintenance tasks.	1
Food Preparation Serving-Related	Preparing and cooking foods and/or serving patrons in dining establishments or other settings. Duties may include checking food quality, mixing drinks/ingredients, cleaning dishware, taking orders, planning menus, and other food/serving-related functions.	1
Personal Care Service	Providing personal assistance, care, and services to individuals in various contexts. Duties may include attending to children, caring for the elderly or disabled, coordinating tourist travel, ensuring safety and comfort to travelers, providing cosmetic services, coordinating recreational activities for residential facilities, as well as other personal care and service tasks.	1

Each book takes you through the Know Thyself Process® in small, easily digestible steps so that these insights become a habit for you.

As a reader of this book, you are entitled to a Book of You™ for a special price of $49.95. Just visit www.bookofyou.com/ebookreader, select the choosing "Choosing a New Career" book from the drop down book menu, and enter the discount code below when ordering.

Use discount code: ebook2016

---

1. Credit to Dan Perry, independent Birkman Method® consultant and frequent trainer for The Birkman Method®, for sharing this analogy.

DR. SARAH E. BROWN

is leading the charge to revolutionize the self-help industry through the power of personalization. Following a very successful career in Corporate America, she recently retired as Managing Director at Accenture to devote herself to personalizing self-help advice in the form of customized books. With a Ph. D. in PsychoEducational Processes, 15 years of Talent Management experience, and skills and experience in scaling complicated operations, she is uniquely qualified to do so.

Her completely personalized books, titled the *Book of You*™, are available at www.bookofyou.com.

Dr. Brown has also joined Jack Canfield, along with a select group of experts and professionals, to co-write the book titled, *The Road to Success: Today's Leading Entrepreneurs and Professionals Reveal Their Step-By-Step Systems To Help You Achieve The Health, Wealth and Lifestyle You Deserve.*

In response to requests from readers and clients, Dr. Brown wrote *Let Your Personality be your Career Guide* to help an individual quickly determine the key personality components that should be considered in choosing a career. It contains a wealth of stories and exercises to help an individual zero in on key interests, strengths and motivational needs that are important in choosing a career in which the reader will be happy, successful, and understood.

A native of Virginia, Dr. Brown resides in Wilmington, Delaware, with her husband and standard poodle, Maharani. When not writing, researching, or speaking, she can be found rowing on the Christina River or chasing Maharani through the woods.